# A Boy's Life Journey

MARK DENDEKKER

NEWMAN SPRINGS PUBLISHING
320 Broad Street
Red Bank, NJ 07701

First originally published by Newman Springs Publishing 2023

ISBN 979-8-88763-407-4 (Paperback)
ISBN 979-8-88763-408-1 (Digital)

Printed in the United States of America

*For Mom. She always had a book in her hand.*

# ACKNOWLEDGMENTS

Like I wrote on the back page, we all need one another's help.

Mom—she was *so* supportive. She got me everywhere I needed to be to play golf. See, I didn't even know what a classroom was, let alone where they might be. Golf was going to have to be my ticket.

Don Sterre, my second biggest fan. He was the athletic director at Santa Monica High School. He got me kicked up a year early to play on the golf team. That was when my game flourished. He was also instrumental in skating me into SDSU.

Dr. Frank "Scotty" Scott. Besides telling me that I needed to go to class, also you will see a difference between your classmates which ones went to college. He was right. It's called an education. Writing and reading are not just a principle; they are "the principle." I would like to thank my university and professors.

As far as the writing and publishing of this book is concerned, Cricket and Brandel, who helped bring paper to pen. Kris and her whole staff at Pryntonics Friday Harbor, who took what I wrote and put it in a format to publish. Mark Duper, a publisher from Tucson who gave me some great tips. Masakayan and Fonda, my two classmates who have filled me with confidence without even trying to.

Susan Percich. I can't even put into words what this woman means to me. Life has thrown me some Major League torpedoes. I said to her, "You have saved my life 'literally' a dozen times." She said, "No, more than that." Thank you, Susan.

Thank you, all of you.

Mark

Look at the size of that mitt! It's bigger than me. That's why
I won two MVPs of Santa Monica baseball. Nothing ever
got by me, the "hot corner" baby. And I never missed the
first baseman even if I had to sidearm it from the dirt.

Gun-for-hire no. 7. I could really shoot, but I
knew basketball was not in my future.

Tell me this boy doesn't look a little wet behind the ears?

Midtwenties in San Diego. The thing I remember about
this picture is that my life was in a really good place.

Tenth tee, Rancho Park. Everyone was trying to
do Jack Nicklaus's reverse *C*. I think I got it.

Mark
DenDekker

Mark DenDekker. Senior picture. Nice tie!

My mom! I love this picture of her.

Mom and me. We really liked each other.

My mother's sixtieth birthday!

Check out those chicken legs!

The 1992 Los Angeles Marathon. Does this guy look happy or what? Nice. Broke three and a half hours.

A picture tells a thousand words. This is the 2005 LA Marathon. Toast. Completely spent, but I closed the deal at forty-two. Right on time!

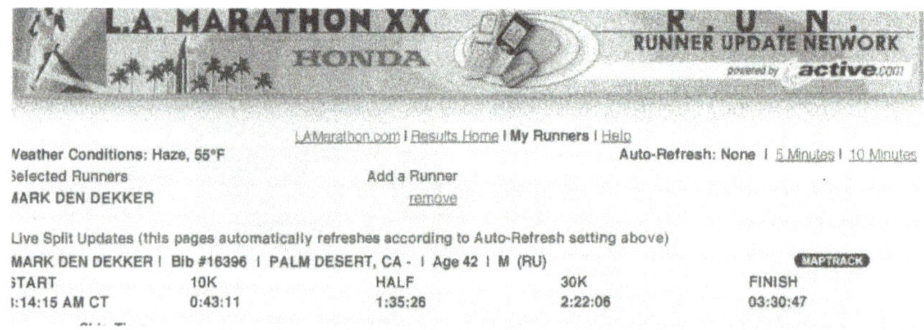

At forty-two, I finished 601st out of twenty-five thousand people. Nice. That includes the Kenyans.

Don't see a lot wrong with this swing. Funny thing is that on my eighteenth birthday, I played in a rainstorm and got really sick. I was down for two weeks. I lost fifteen pounds. This picture was taken right after I finally got out of bed.

Sixteen years old, on the driving range at Riviera Country Club. It was taken for our school log. Purina.

Look at that hair… Me winning the SoCal P.G.A junior championship. Does this kid look like he just came off the beach, or what? Nice.

The year 1989. Well, you can tell where this is. Nice picture, rough week.

Sydney 1989. On the left, you have Tim Loustalot; and
on the right, "Crocodile Dundee." Nice hat.

Redemption 1990. What a great week. I finished ninth. I had paid
for this trip well before I left. I was in an all-inclusive hotel. I was
eating steak and lobster all week. The saying on the mini tours was
"Eat hamburger, play like hamburger. Eat steak, play like steak."

Freshman year, no. 2 team at Torrey Pines. Lawrence Zech, Bob Madsen, Scotty, Mike Davidson, me, Bob Levin, and Doug Potter.

Me in my dad's office. He actually had a genius IQ. He also was off his rocker. Some of the greatest minds are in a state of mental illness. I will always feel sorry for him. He did not have a very happy life.

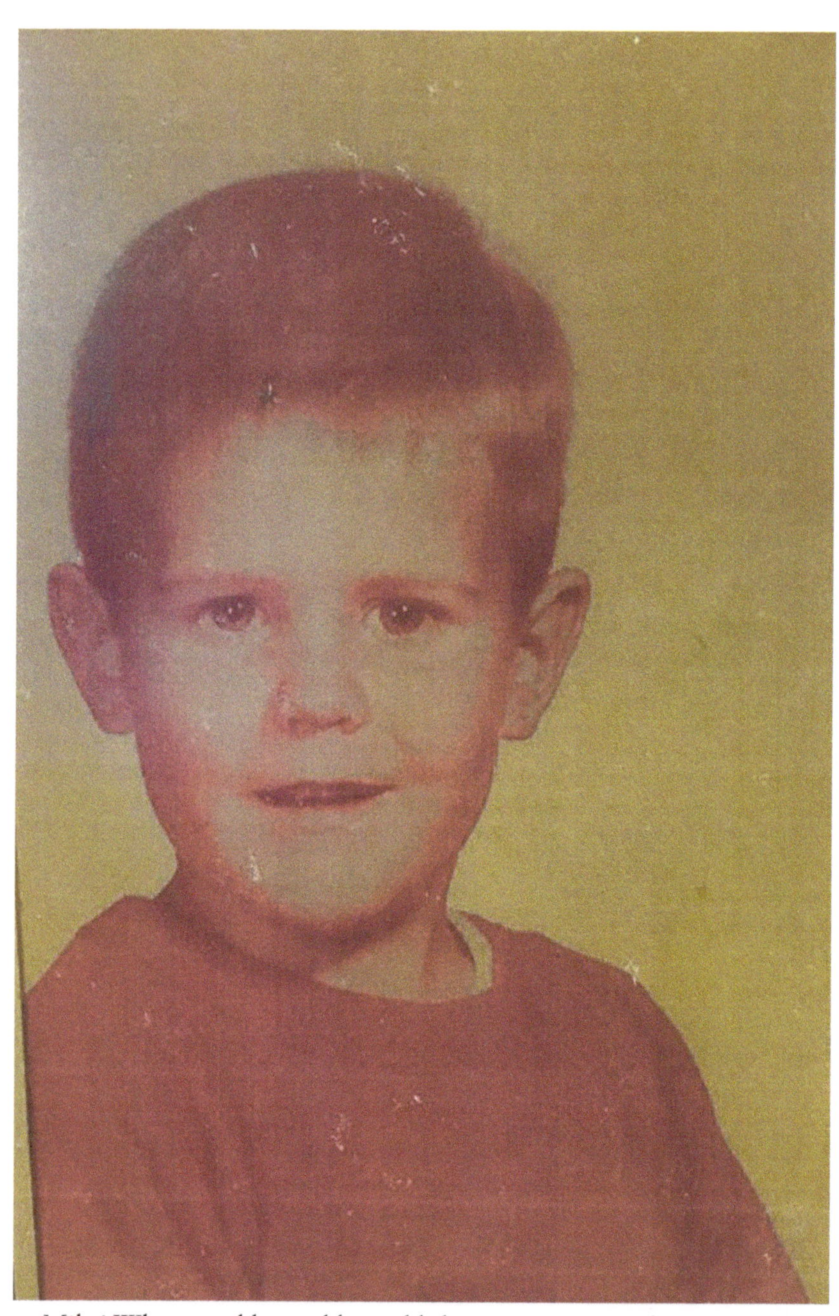

Mike! What possible trouble could these two innocent boys get into?

Fuzzy winning the Masters. I think Mike was right. I could
have taken him at Riviera. It was my home course!

Amelia Earhart A.K.A. Susan, or the other way around.
Not, many people know Amelia had a navigator in the back
of the plane. Susan has always been my co-pilot.

# SAN DIEGO STATE MEN'S GOLF RECORD BOOK

## INDIVIDUAL TOURNAMENT CHAMPIONS

| Year | Player | Tournament |
|---|---|---|
| 1948 | Frank Morley | CCAA Championship |
| 1950 | Gene Littler | CCAA Championship |
| 1951 | Frank Morley | CCAA Championship |
| 1952 | Don Love | CCAA Championship |
| 1955 | Marvin Braddock | CCAA Championship |
| 1960 | Ron O'Connor | Western Intercollegiate |
| 1960 | Ron O'Connor | So. California Intercollegiate |
| 1960 | Chuck Courtney | CCAA Championship |
| 1962 | Alan Campbell | CCAA Championship |
| 1964 | Alan Campbell | CCAA Championship |
| 1964 | Alan Campbell | CSU Los Angeles Invitational |
| 1965 | Alan Campbell | So. California Championship |
| 1966 | Mike Riley | Fresno Classic |
| 1966 | Mike Riley | So. California Championship |
| 1970 | Jim Bradford | CSU Los Angeles Invitational |
| 1971 | Jack Spradlin | So. California Championship |
| 1971 | Jack Spradlin | CSU Los Angeles Invitational |
| 1972 | Tom Minor | Vandenberg Invitational |
| 1972 | Lon Hinkle | Fresno Classic |
| 1972 | Lon Hinkle | PCAA Championships |
| 1976 | Lennie Clements | PCAA Championships |
| 1976 | Terry Raymer | UC Riverside Invitational |

| 1976 | Curt Worley | Aztec Invitational |
| 1976 | Curt Worley | UCSB Invitational |
| 1977 | Gerry Simoni | U.S. Intercollegiate |
| 1978 | Lennie Clements | Gary Sanders Memorial |
| 1978 | Lennie Clements | UC Riverside Invitational |
| 1978 | Lennie Clements | Sun Devil Invitational |
| 1978 | Curt Worley | Sun Devil Invitational |
| 1978 | Rick Gordon | PCAA Championships |
| 1978 | Curt Worley | Aztec Invitational |
| 1979 | Lennie Clements | U.S. Intercollegiate |
| 1981 | Barry Mahlberg | So. California Championship |
| 1982 | Scott Williams | Sun Devil Invitational |
| 1982 | Greg Twiggs | So. California Championship |
| 1983 | Greg Twiggs | Arizona Conquistador |
| 1983 | Greg Twiggs | Pac Coast Classic |
| 1983 | Greg Twiggs | UCSB Invitational |
| 1983 | Kris Moe | Western Intercollegiate |
| 1983 | Kris Moe | Aztec Invitational |
| 1984 | Kris Moe | USIU Invitational |
| 1984 | Kris Moe | Pacific Coast Intercollegiate |
| 1984 | Mark DenDekker | SD Golf Academy Intercollegiate |
| 1985 | Howard Johnson | Sun Devil Invitational |
| 1986 | Mark DenDekker | USD Invitational |
| 1987 | Scott Almquist | USD Invitational |
| 1988 | Bill Coleman | USD Invitational |
| 1988 | Bill Coleman | CS Stanislaus Invitational |
| 1990 | Kevin Riley | Grand Canyon Invitational |

Current golfers are in **bold**.

Not a lot of guys were winning multiple tournaments. It's a nice list to be on. The year 1984 really hurt. Kris Moe and I were winning and making each other better right up until I got fired. We were a really good team. Too bad we didn't get to see how good were could have been.

Intake/Output Summary (Last 24 hours) at 05/03/18 0638
Last data filed at 05/03/18 0550

|  | **Gross per 24 hour** |
|---|---|
| Intake | 525 ml |
| Output | 3175 ml |
| **Net** | -2650 ml |

GENERAL: Alert and oriented.

LUNGS: Clear from the anterior bilateral.

HEART: Regular rhythm. The patient has a grade 1/6 systolic murmur heard best at the apex of his heart no diastolic.

ABD: His liver is palpable at the right costal margin. I do not appreciate nodularity. It is nontender. His spleen is not palpable.

EXT: The patient's necrosis is relatively superficial on the skin. The patient has no significant necrosis of the remaining fascia or muscle. The patient has no smell to his wound.

SKIN: The patient has no other specific skin rash.

<u>Lab data:</u>

Recent Labs

|       | 05/02/18 0610 | 05/02/18 0005 | 05/02/18 0001 |
|-------|------|------|------|
| WBC   | 13.0* | -- | 15.4* |
| HGB   | 12.1* | 13.3* | 13.0* |
| HCT   | 33.3* | 39 | 36.6* |
| PLT   | 95* | -- | 99* |
| NA    | 129* | 124* | -- |
| K     | 3.4 | 3.6 | -- |
| CL    | 90* | 85* | -- |
| CO2   | 24 | 22* | -- |
| BUN   | 10 | 8.0 | -- |
| CR    | 0.74* | 0.9 | -- |

The word that comes to mind is *ouch*! I wrote an acknowledgment page, but "master surgeon" Dr. Peter Galpin gets an all-star billing. The fact that he saved my foot, leg, and my life with this mess? What a skilled and talented man. I thank the Lord every day that our paths crossed.

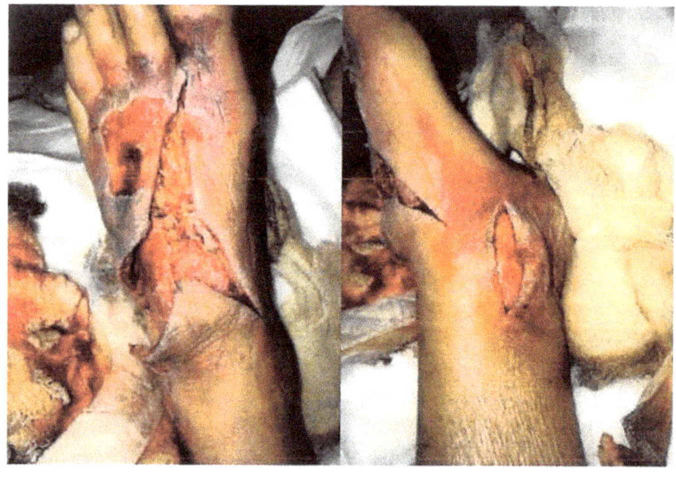

* ⭐ *

# INTRODUCTION

I think that the best way to read this book is to have an understanding of where I come from.

I grew up in Southern California, did junior golf, and played on the same college team as a guy named Dennis Paulson. One time he said to me, "You are a rebel without a cause." Now I am not sure about that. I always thought I had a cause.

It all started when I was twelve, specifically the day that I went to Riviera to caddy. Shortly after being hired, I was fired for hanging out in the clubhouse. I didn't get the concept that my buddies were members and I was a caddy, a second-class citizen. That's when I developed a complete lack of respect for authority. Mike Jones and I had that in common. Frankly, I still don't and never will. I was about fourteen or fifteen when I realized that it does not matter what <u>anybody</u> thinks. The only opinion that matters is the one of the man upstairs.

Over the years, people have heard my stories and said, "You should write a book." Well, English was never my strong suit, so much so that my last two classes were freshman English. I was twenty-three, and everyone else was eighteen—pretty funny. It was one of the best things to happen to me. Even when you finish all your classes, you have to pass something called the upper-division writing exam to graduate. A lot of people had to take it multiple times. I aced it. It has always stuck with me. I have always written letters. The thought of writing a book has always been in my head. Well, I went to Hawaii looking for work during COVID-19 and got quarantined in Hilo, Hawaii. I met this gal aka Cricket the first night at a retreat called Birds and Blossoms. Sidenote: It should have been called

Hurricane Central. I found out the hard way that Hilo is America's rainiest city. Cricket said, "Tell me a story." I literally had nothing to do and started writing. The funny thing is that I held on to these pictures. I thought that if I lost them, I would lose myself. If nothing else, I had a great time writing it!

The Brandel Chamblee factor: I grew up in LA, where everyone is famous! The only other person I have approached is Charles Barkley. I love that guy. He gave me a bear hug. "I never felt *so* small!" and he said, "Feel the love, baby!" Nice.

So as you will find out in the book, I caught something called necrotizing fasciitis. If you read the book, you will find out how insane what and how it happened. Homeless, broke, and crippled—not the trifecta you are looking for.

I'm living in Lāhainā park in Maui, just learning to walk again. It's outdoor seating at the Pioneer Inn. Brandel is sitting by himself, and I think that is odd. I know that he played at Texas when I was at SDSU. I start telling him funny stories about people and places that I knew he was familiar with. I have his full attention. He asks me what I am doing, and I tell him about the disease. He is shocked. He never heard of it before. I hadn't either until I was living it. Brandel and Cricket, here we go!

# MY STORY

My story starts at eight years old. That's when I met Mike Jones and found sports. The Boys & Girls Club of Santa Monica was fantastic for biddy basketball. My nickname was Hot Dog. I threw it up from everywhere. They could not get mad at me because I made everything! I scored fifty points in one game. In flag football, I played quarterback; and when I turned thirteen, I knew I was out of my league. Up until twelve years old, it is about athletic ability, then it becomes about size. I knew that I would never be big enough to play football or basketball.

Baseball was my passion. Little League Baseball in Santa Monica was fantastic. It was for those eight years of age to twelve. Everyone's families would come out for the games. That's where Mike and I met at age eight. We became inseparable. It was really a fun time. Mike lived with his dad, Jim, who really liked me; and I lived with my mom, Carmen, who really liked Mike.

When I was eleven and twelve, I won MVP of Santa Monica Little League as a third baseman. Third basemen usually don't win MVP awards unless your name is Brooks Robinson or Mike Schmidt. That was where everything started getting wild

One day at the Boys & Girls Club, one of the supervisors said, "You want to go play golf?" Why not! It was a par 3 called Santa Monica Shores. It hasn't existed since they built condos. I was smitten! So this was where golf started to get funny. After about a dozen rounds, he said to me, "Let's take a day trip to San Diego and play Torrey Pines." Sure!

So we headed out onto Torrey Pines South Course—big mistake. It was a cold, wet morning like it usually was. I just remember trying to hack it out of that deep, wet, thick rough. I don't think I broke 120. I remember the couple of hours' drive home.

I was <u>so</u> discouraged. Why would anyone want to play this game? I would eventually learn to play that course well.

So at this point, things on the baseball front were getting ugly! After the MVP season at age twelve, it was time for all-stars. One day in practice, from the centerfield wall, I threw a strike. So the coach for the all-star team gets a "brilliant idea" and makes me the starting pitcher. I knew absolutely <u>nothing</u> about pitching! I got rocked for twelve runs. So that ended my Little League career.

The next year was PONY League. For some reason, they still had me pitching that day. Pam Detrihxe was the first girl to play. She also was my first girlfriend. I was *so* nervous I beaned her. Everyone thought I did it on purpose, but I didn't. That is the last thing I remember about my baseball career.

At this point, it was summer, and I was thirteen. My grandmother was the head housekeeper at Murrieta Hot Springs. She gave my mom a break and took me for the summer.

Well, I had nothing to do, so I ended up playing fifty-four holes a day. I had found Rancho Park in West Los Angeles. The guys were shocked. I left shooting in the nineties and came back shooting par. At that point, I became totally focused on golf.

The year I was fourteen was a big year for me. I won the SoCal PGA championship for the 12–14 division and a trip to Florida for the nationals. The morning of the first round, I was yelling at my mother. I thought she washed my clubs. They were soaking wet. I had no experience with humidity. I didn't make it past the third hole. I literally could not hold on to the club. Still, I wasn't discouraged.

Lincoln Junior High School was grades 7–9, and SaMoHi was grades 10–12. All the other schools in our league—Palos Verdes, Rolling Hills, Beverly Hills, etc.—were four-year high schools. Don Steere, the athletic director, got me kicked up to high school early.

I had *so* much fun that spring. There were five seniors and me, a freshman. I played no. 2 behind Jim Detrihxe. Jimmy was (is) a great player. He made it to two Broadmore finals and "the "show":

the 1991 US Open. He's a really nice guy too. I was the little brother to these guys. After every match, we had a pile on the last green. Somehow, I was always at the bottom. Those were really fun times.

The next year, Mike came up. Mike played no. 2, which was cool because we always played together. It seemed like in every match, I shot thirty-five, and Mike thirty-nine. We played nine-hole matches. During senior year, our team was so bad. Pomona National won the CIF team title. No individual title. I didn't care. I just wanted to play. Mike choose not to go. I shot sixty-seven, thirty, on the back nine. Nobody else broke ninety. When I was a senior, I was playing great. I kept getting better every year of high school. I qualified for Junior World at sixteen. Uн-oн! In Torrey Pines South Course, I put four decent rounds together. I would get my revenge on that course later, sort of! I was one of the best juniors in the country. I had won a handful of tournaments, and most importantly, I beat Sam Randolph by three shots for a return trip to the PGA National Junior Championship in Florida, which was the hardest junior tournament to qualify for. There is only one spot in the 12–14 and 15–17 divisions. I didn't play well in Florida but managed to complete four rounds. Off to San Diego State.

Rancho Park. We had a crew that was totally obsessed with the game. Among the cast of characters were Mac O'Grady, Greg Twiggs, and Tony Sills—three future PGA Tour winners. Also worth mentioning were Larry Salk and Gil Zaharoni, two great guys. There are lots of great stories but too many to tell. What fun.

So here is big lesson number 2. We would show up at sunrise and play all day and then hit the night-lit driving range. One evening, Mac and Twiggy were holding court on the bottom far right tee. It was only 250 yards to the back fence, but it was a hundred feet high. So these two goofballs were hitting drivers off the deck the cement! They were hitting towering cut shots over the back fence. These guys were twice my size. I went home depressed. I knew that I would physically not ever be able to hit that shot. Kinda like in basketball and football, these guys were just bigger and stronger. This is a lesson that anyone who has ever played any sport should learn. Zach Johnson won the 2007 Masters. The whole week, he never went for a par 5 in two. He beat these guys by stuffing a wedge down their throat! Golf is lines and angles—geometry. I learned how to hit a humming draw that would hit and take off like a scolded cat! It would roll right up next to the big boys. Actually, in college, I had a black-dot Ping 1 iron. I could hit that thing over three hundred yards. It was nicknamed by my teammates the atomic 1 iron. It was like the Energizer Bunny; that thing would hit and just keep running!

Mike and me are a formula for destruction! We absolutely wreaked havoc on the Los Angeles Country Clubs. See, we were dangerous. We had *so* many factors working in our favor. First of all, the times—it was a different era.

There was no war. Things were laid back. There was minimal security and even more than that <u>nobody</u> was doing what we were doing. Nobody had any idea what we were doing! Haha! It went like this. We snuck into almost every country club in Los Angeles. We *so* much had the audacity to go into the dining room and sign for lunch. Also, the pro shop was fair game! Need some balls, a new glove maybe? Just sign for it. All the clubs had reciprocal chits, and nobody was checking! For example, Mark Johnson, Bel-Air Country Club membership number 1462—bingo! Never got caught. We dressed and acted the part with total confidence. The big thing was that we had a safety net. We were minors. It all ended on our eighteenth birthdays. We weren't stupid. We had a hell of a run! Far and away among the clubs, LACC was our favorite target. We played more than the members, about three or four days a week for years.

Behind the second tee of the north course was a school with a very hoppable fence. The funny thing is that it was in the heart of the city, and it was a complete forest. Most of the time, we wouldn't even see one person. It was extremely hilly as well. That was why we gave up caddying there. These members had huge bags, and we would be packing double. One guy would be hooking it, and the other guy would have a slice. We would come home like we had been in a prize fight. As far as playing there is concerned, we looked and dressed the part. We hit good shots and blended right in. Plus, there was no marshal.

The year I was seventeen was the best year of my life to date. My uncle John Wortmann gave me a car. I was dating the best-looking girl in school, and in Mike I had the best wingman ever. We never got caught. I think that was why we had the confidence: we had each other's backs. I also was playing the best golf I have, maybe ever.

My uncle John was always good to me. He was a great man. In my Rancho days, I met Buzz Greene through Mike's dad, Jim. Buzz might be the best putter I have ever seen. Jim and Buzz had just bought memberships at a new club in Thousand Oaks called North Ranch Country Club. On Saturday and Sundays mornings, I would drive Coast Highway from Santa Monica through Malibu and shoot through the canyons into Thousand Oaks. The car John gave me was a Ford Capri (had a V6 engine). I don't how smart it was to give a seventeen-year-old boy a car like that! That thing could fly! I was treated like a member and usually came home with a pocket full of cash. Life was about to get more complicated and more difficult. I had a fantastic childhood. Thanks, Mom.

To follow are four short stories of those years.

# PLAYBOY MANSION WEST

As I stated before, LACC North was our home course, unbeknownst to them. So to set the stage for this, Hugh Hefner's Playboy Mansion West sits right off the fourteenth tee. Mike and I were always peeking over the wall, looking for Bunnies. We were sixteen, for God's sake! Boys! Eventually, we would hop the wall a couple of times, but that was as far as we ventured.

Well, one night (late evening), I was playing with Scott Karlow. We decided to take it to another level. At the mansion, in the backyard, was something called the grotto. It was connected to the pool, an underground cave. It was full of whirlpools, Jacuzzis, and furniture that was designed for sex. We found HH robes, cigars, and a refrigerator full of Heinekens. We were looking for bunnies! We screwed around in there for an hour or so. We were smart enough not to go to the main house. On the other side of the house was a game room. It had a full refrigerator and more Heinekens! After an hour or so, I thought it was time to go.

That was when security nabbed us. These guys called the cops, but they were laughing. I was looking around the office and saw, like, twenty cameras. They saw the whole thing. I guess they just let us run loose for a while. So the cops showed up, and they were laughing! They took us to the station and called our parents. Guess what? They were trying not to laugh! We were minors, so no charges were filed. In the years that followed, my mother loved telling that story. My mother and I were best friends. She let me run loose. She knew how to handle me. I never let her down. I was <u>always</u> what I needed to be when I was supposed to be.

✦

# A NIGHT AT BRENTWOOD COUNTRY CLUB

It was Friday. That meant poker night, same time as "Fuzzy and cocktails." So we always had a supply of party favors—cigarettes, blow, and booze. The game ended early, and one of the cast of characters, Scott Karlow, informed us that he had cable cutters. Brentwood was down the street, and we decided to cut into the cart barn and go for a joyride. We grabbed the rest of the beer, and off we went.

We were all over the course, playing bumper cars, running over flatsticks, and just causing general chaos. Two guys got stuck in a bunker, and they went back for fresh carts. Haha! The snack shack "was" a little wooden hut. I had the ingenious idea for all of us to line up from a different angle and hit it at the same time. *Bam!* Leveled it! At this point, we were starting to lose participants. Scott cut open the back gate. Scott took off.

Now there were three: Mike, David Pardo, and me. We headed off for Wilshire Boulevard. Now I was thinking we might be pushing this a little far. Ya think?

So we started heading back to the course. At the corner of Twenty-Sixth and Montana, Dave got his cart stuck between a stone wall and a lamppost. We were trying to get it free when a police helicopter came in right over our heads. I yelled, "Scatter!" and we all went off in different directions. I personally jumped about six backyard fences and dove under a bush. I stayed there for a couple of hours.

Saturday was caddy day at Brentwood. We showed up, and there was Mike. At this point, we were hoping Dave skated. It was bad! It looked like a war zone. The members were fuming! Mike and I were trying to keep a straight face. It was okay; the members had plenty of money to fix it. There is a thing called the statute of limitations, right?

That is not the end of the story. One of our buddies delivered us the beer from the local liquor store at the corner. Well, they found the receipt on the golf course. The FBI showed up at our buddy's house, Roger Cohn. His dad said he had been with him all night. I am sure that with Roger being a minor, his Dad knew it would be his ass that was at the end of it. Haha, we did not see Roger for a month!

# COCKTAILS AND FUZZY

It was the late '70s, and there was a lot of extracurricular activities going on, mostly cocaine and alcohol. It was the 1979 Glen Campbell Los Angeles Open at Riviera. Mike and I were sixteen and in "full flight." Sunday came around, and we were off to Riviera. Of course, we didn't pay; we knew twenty ways to sneak into that track. Turns out my mother's employer, Great Western Savings, had a corporate tent right behind the eighteenth green. Mike and I were in the tent for hours, getting loaded on screwdrivers. Like I said, it was a different time. It was such a fun and loose time. Nobody ever heard of *politically correct* or would have cared!

Cool! I was only twenty feet away from Lanny Wadkins when he knocked in the winning putt. The pun was in the back left corner, right where the tent was.

Just a sidenote, Lanny would win the Players Championship that year. Boy, that guy was intimidating! He was like a buzz saw. You did not want that guy breathing down your neck!

The tournament was over, but Mike and I were just getting started. I was not hard. We snuck into the clubhouse and found our way to the suites upstairs. It was very small. There were five people: two guys talking in the corner, the bartender, and Fuzzy with some gal. We ordered some screwdrivers and started talking to Fuzzy. Fuzzy had just won San Diego as a rookie to qualify for the Masters. I don't remember much of the conversation except that Mike kept telling him I could kick his ass over and over again and that he needed to be here in the morning. The other thing I remember was Fuzzy. What an awesome guy. He was having so much fun, playing along. Just a few weeks later, he won the Masters.

# THE SHOT

This is how this story goes. It's still hard to believe this actually happened.

It was my senior year at Santa Monica High School. As I said earlier, I was playing great golf! One of a handful of players in the state, Ron Rhoads, was not only the head pro at Riv; he was also the head coach for USC's golf team. Somehow, Santa Monica got Riv as a home course. Even though he had fired me months before, I got to play the course because of my school.

Just being the brat that I was, I thought I would bust his balls one day. Right before a match, I asked him for a word. We sat on the steps to the pro shop. I asked him for a scholarship to SC. The answer was no. See, I knew this guy hated me. I just wanted him to say no.

Twenty minutes later, we are on the first tee.

Ron showed up with a member for a playing lesson. So they teed off in front of us. Well, we played holes 1 and 2 and proceeded to hole 3, which was a par 4, 440 yards dead into the afternoon wind coming off the ocean.

I hit a good drive into the center of the fairway. The three other players had already played their second shots short of the green. Ron was still on the green with the member. He saw me standing alone in the fairway two hundred yards out. He waved me up. With the wind blowing, it was playing, like, 250 or 260. I pulled out the "atomic 1 iron." I was standing over the shot, ready to pull the trigger, and a thought went through my head. It was a very small green with a large bunker in front. I was thinking, *I can't carry the bunker and stop it on the green.* So I went back to the bag and pulled out a 3 wood. I figured I could hit it higher and stop it faster.

Well, I hit this thing as pure as the driven snow! A frozen rope right at the flatstick—I knew that I couldn't see it hit. I reached down for my bag and started walking down the fairway. Ron was going nuts! He was jumping up and down like a pogo stick. It took a second to comprehend. I canned it! He was like "You should have seen it! It hit five feet short of the hole, took a little hop, and went in dead center!"

I was thinking, *Should I say, "Do I get a scholarship now?"* I knew that it would not change anything. I really didn't want to go to SC. I was off to SDSU. Over the years that followed, a lot of guys on the USC team asked me about that story. And I just said that Ron wouldn't lie.

✦ ★ ✦

# PRELUDE TO COLLEGE

I think that to best understand what happened in college is to know of the events leading up to it. Buzz Greene and I loved playing together. We really respected each other's game. He was a phenomenal putter. Ask anyone. He made everything, and I mean <u>everything</u>! One time, he holed a shot out of a lake. The rule of thumb on that is that it can't be more than halfway submerged, which it was. That was the kind of player he was. You could <u>never</u> count him out of a hole. Buzz played for Dr. Frank Scott at SDSU in the early '70s. Scotty was a legend. Everybody loved Scotty. I believe he was Gene Littler's coach. Gene won the 1961 US Open. That tells you how long. Someone told me he was the first coach elected into the college golf hall of fame.

San Diego State was my <u>only</u> option. Along with the "bad boy" reputation, I had a 2.1 grade point average. I never went to school.

I was busy at the golf course and barely got out. Scotty pulled me aside and said, "Mark, your SAT score is outstanding, and your grade point average is horrible. If you want to play golf here, you need to go to class." Golf wasn't a fall sport for us, so I took eighteen units and got, like, a 3.6 or 3.7 GPA. I coasted that all the way to graduation. After that, I got a C in almost every class I took—good enough. He was a wonderful influence on me.

Back to high school, we had the CIF state tournament at the end of the year. In my junior campaign, I finished third and almost won at Rancho Sante Fe in San Diego. The tournament had the coolest format. About fifty of us qualified for finals. At finals, only the top ten players got to play the second round. We were at Bakersfield

Country Club. I shot seventy-three to finish right on the number. The good news is that seventy was leading—only three back.

Something happened that day. I can't explain it. Whatever I had, I lost it that day.

I came home in eighty-two. I thought I was going to win. It felt like all the air was let out. This was <u>not</u> the way I saw my high school career ending!

I don't remember much of that summer. I was too old for junior golf and could not afford amateur golf.

I remember clearly the day my mother drove me to the dorms. It was the fall of '81. I was the happiest guy on the planet, Disneyland times ten! My mother, on the other hand, had a petrified look on her face! Here we go!

# COLLEGE

It was the fall of '81. We didn't play. Golf was a spring sport. I remember going to the SDSU-versus-BYU football game with Twiggy Greg and was playing no. 1, and he was telling me that I was going to be no. 2. I did not have the heart to tell him that I had lost my confidence.

It was the spring of '81—golf season. We played ten or twelve rounds of qualifying. I had to go to a thirty-six-hole playoff for the twelfth and final spot. I made it by one shot. I got to play in a couple of tournaments on SDSU's no. 2 team. I played altogether awful! I only remember two incidences. My game was gone. My first competitive round was at Shadowridge Country Club in San Diego. I posted eighty-eight. Nice. The other was at USC's tournament at, of all places, North Ranch Country Club. We sent two teams.

Somehow we were paired with SC's no. 1 team. I, of all people, was paired with Sam Randolph. Uh-oh. We had some good battles in junior and high school golf. Sam played some amazing golf in college. Off the first tee, I hit a hosel rocket with a driver. That was a shank. It almost hit me! It went straight up and to the embankment and back down to the ladies' tee—kinda embarrassing! Shot seventy-six was a minor miracle. The end of the season could not come fast enough.

Off the course, oh my God. Every night was a party! Even though I wasn't playing well, I was having a great time.

In the second year, I made a smart move. Red shirt. I was totally lost. I don't remember much of that year except that somehow, I found my confidence again. Heading into my sophomore season, I was playing well again. Funny thing is that in all the years I played golf, I played very well at times and very poorly at times. Ready! John Erickson was right—total-feel player.

It was now my sophomore season. Well, the qualifying could not have gone any better. I smoked everyone hands down, no. 1. I was looking and thinking that the All-Americans won two tournaments to start on track. In two minutes, my season was over.

We were playing a tournament at Shadow Ridge again. It was fifty-four holes, and I posted up sixty-eight. On the third nine, I was three under and leading by a lot. The last hole, the ninth, was a short par 4 with a lake in front of the green where the pin was cut. I proceeded to put four balls in the water and skull the fifth in the back bunker. Now, the clubhouse sat right off the green. Everyone was standing there, waiting for us to finish. I turned around and helicoptered my wedge at the can. I mean, I whirlybirded that thing as hard as I could at the can. It was an explosion.

The previous year, Scotty retired. The new coach was a man named Tag Merritt (he was cut from the same cloth as Ron Rhoads). He despised me. I was promptly shit-canned, fired. What I thought was unfair was that he never said one word to me. Scotty would have sat me down.

I could just hear Scotty saying, "Now, Mark, you looked pretty stupid out there," and I would be like "You're right. I won't make the same mistake. Sorry." I would be sincere. Thing is that what made me a loose cannon is what also made me good at times. In the next couple of years, we had a new coach every year, but none of them were good. By my senior season, the team was in shambles. I was the only guy breaking eighty. The good news for me was that Tag did not come back one and done.

This is a good place to talk about life off the course.

I'm really proud of my college degree. I worked really hard to get it! Talk about a full plate! I was taking a full academic schedule, working in a restaurant thirty hours a week, and totally committed to golf and the golf program. Of course, partying came first. Haha!

Scotty had a great recruiting tactic. He would walk around campus with us in the summertime. All the girls were hardly wearing any clothes. Sold! My school! I remember my mother saying, "Sometime, everyone will be going to the beach, and you will have to stay home and study." Nuh-uh, no way. I was the first guy on the bus. See, I figured something out. You didn't have to study! I _never_ missed a class. I also sat in the front row. See, these professors had big egos. I knew what they wanted to hear. Slam dunk!

Life off the course was wild, but that changed one very sad day.

It was June '85. The Boston Celtics had the no. 2 pick in the draft and picked Len Bias from Maryland. They were already loaded with Len as the icing on the cake.

Two days later, the world was in shock. He died from a cocaine overdose. In the late '70s and early '80s, everybody was snorting cocaine. I mean _everybody_! It was like a dinner cocktail. Nobody was shooting or smoking it. Harmless, right? The world changed that day for most of us. We got a real sobering reality of how dangerous this was.

There are a few things that are hard to write about this is one. We lost Pam Detrihxe at this time to this insidious drug. She was _so_ pretty, intelligent, and funny and a very wonderful person. Mike said it best. She was in a bad place at a bad time. It did one positive thing: it woke everybody up.

It was my junior year, and we had another knucklehead new coach. We had a pretty good team. Dennis was playing no. 1, Howie Johnson no. 2, I no. 3, Mike Foley no. 4, and Mark Mason no. 5. Mark qualified for the US Open a few years later. Nice.

This was a great time. Everybody had their guns! UC Irvine had Eric Woods and Perry Parker; Pacific had Jeff Wilson and Jeff Brehaut; USIU had Bryan Gorman (best swing ever); Long Beach State had Doug Garwood and Paul Goydos; USC had Sammy Randolph and Brian Henninger; and Fresno State was loaded with Tim Loustalot, John Erickson, and the Sutherland brothers—Kevin and David. And then there was UCLA, which was in another league with Duffy Waldorf and too many great players to mention. Oh yea, there was Scott McCannon, but he didn't make the team! It was a fun year. My game was up and down more than ever. As a team, we sucked for the talent we had. Two tournaments stick out, both in Arizona. In Tucson National, I ponied up seventy-four, seventy-one. Doesn't sound great, but the conditions were tough. I was only two shots off the lead. In the last round, I played with Billy Mayfair, "Mister Arizona." I knew him from junior golf. He's another one of the really good guys. I shot seventy-nine. It still hurts.

So we showed up at McCormick Ranch, ASU's tourney. The only reason we were in the field was Scotty's legacy. Everybody was there including Oklahoma State no. 1 team in the country. They took five out of six scores every day. I posted eighty—snowman. Throw out! You never want to be thrown out because you have to eat dinner with these guys. Something about this week was that the wind was blowing twenty to thirty miles per hour all week. Par was a great score this week. This tournament was so big that they were posting nine-hole scores. On the second day, I shot forty on the first nine. Halfway to eighty, right? Well, I posted up the best nine holes I ever played in college: thirty-two, four under in a windstorm. Seventy-two—it put us in the lead of the whole tournament. Funny thing is that I finished on nine. Nobody was there except Dennis. Dennis and I grew up together and were always at odds on and off the golf course. So I could see the steam coming out of his ears. Eighty, right? No, seventy-two par. It was a great moment for me. He just stood there with this blank look on his face.

In the last round, at the turn, we were still in the lead. We got Fresno State and UCLA breathing down our necks! Everyone on our team was playing well. The last hole was a par 4 with a pond in front. There was a dead downwind. Of course, the pin was cut right in front. There was also a slope so huge that anything short would come back in the water. Nobody had that shot! We all bogeyed, no doubles—not a crime.

As for me, there was no surprise. Thinking of my meltdown at Shadow Ridge the previous year, I blew it in the back bunker. We finished T2 with UCLA one shot behind Fresno State, 1,141 to 1,142. In the last group, John Erickson striped two shots into the center of the green.

We came home heroes and made the front-page news. Unlike like my senior year of high school, which was such a downer, this season ended great.

It was senior season. Wow! So much happened that year and also didn't. Guess what? We had a new coach: some knucklehead from Western Michigan. Our team was horrible. Even though I had issues with Dennis and Howie, at least I could count on them. College was a team game.

I came out on total fire! Two early wins and one round, and I was eight under through eleven holes. Nobody did that except Sam Randolph. I was labeled "atomic 1 iron and assault on par" and again on track for All-American.

Again, things changed in a very small amount of time.

Let's go back to Torrey Pines South Course. Just writing this, I realize that somehow, it was always the same people and the same courses. Well, we were playing in a USD tourney that was thirty-six holes. I shot seventy-one on the first day, and seventy was the lead. I came out focused and played one shot at a time. I fired thirty-five, one under, going out. On the tenth tee, Randy Lyon showed up. He had replaced Ron Rhoads as USC's coach.

This was lesson no. 3. He asked what my score was. He knew. He said, "You are leading the tournament." He knew exactly what he was doing. I was playing shot to shot, which is what you should always do. I started thinking about it. Then I bogeyed 10, 11, and 12; shot seventy-four; and finished fourth. Doug Garwood won that tournament, seventy-two, sixty-nine. Nice playing, Doug. There are only a few people that I have met that everybody liked. Doug would be one of those. It was not Randy's fault. It was mine. I should have never let it get to me. My season, for some reason, was over. It's a team game. I had an idiot for a coach, and no one else on the team could break eighty. It's sad that it took only three years for those assholes to destroy what Scotty built over decades. Apparently, guys like Xander Schauffele, Scott Piercy, and J. J. Spaun have restored the program. It's a great program. Thanks, guys. Scotty thanks you.

My college golf career was over, but I still needed to finish school. It turned out that I had three classes left to take. Somehow we were all screwed up. That if you don't finish on time, you are a failure is stupid! The rule is that if you are within fifteen units of graduating, you can participate in the ceremony. Here comes the worst decision of my life (well, the second-worst). I was only nine units off, but I was not finished! After everything I went through, it should have been the best day of my life. It was the worst.

It's funny. It ended on a bleak December day. It was depressing! My last class was a brutal upper-division economics class, and all I needed was a D to graduate. It was all about the final. They posted your score on the door by your SS number, and you needed 240 to pass. My score was 241. Just like everything else, I had to make interesting. I walked out of that business building without another person in sight. Wow. How appropriate!

Over.

* ⭐ *

# PRO

First of all, I had no business going pro. It's kinda like what Susan did when she got her master's from San Luis Obispo. She didn't have anything better to do. Off the golf course, I got married. You can probably figure out how that worked out. I then got a job at the Cheesecake Factory in Marina del Rey. What a great group of people. Everybody was an actor, singer, artist, athlete, etc. What a great thing my mom did. She put me in Los Angeles. Whatever you wanted to be was available.

I met Bob Mark in elementary school. His name makes me laugh. See, one time, Mike and I were approached by "America's Finest" Joke what a joke. The guy said to me, "What is your name?"

"Mark DenDekker."

Then they asked Mike Jones.

"Haha," the cop says. "Yeah, and I'm Bob Smith."

I was like "No, really, his name is Mike Jones."

Back to Bob. He is an actor but likes golf. The first week we met, he said, "You play golf?"

"Sure."

"Let's dawn patrol at Rancho Park."

"Great!"

I shot sixty-eight, but the thing was that I had no fives on the card, just threes and fours. Sixteen, I bogeyed no harm. It was a par 3. Eighteen was a par 5 that I could hit in two. Seventeen was the key. It was a legitimate three-shot par 5. I hit a one-hundred-yard wedge shot to a foot. It's the only time I can think of when I'm asked if I have done that on a real, legitimate golf course.

Hey, funny story. Bob and I were playing dawn patrol at Rancho one morning, and he showed up in all yellow. I had to give him a ride home, and when he pulled down the passenger-side visor, a banana landed in his lap. The day before, I went to the car wash and had a Mr. Banana Guy air freshener. It was 05- or 06-, and Sergio Garcia showed up in the hunt on the last day of the British Open, dressed in all yellow, even his shoes! No way the golfing gods were going to let him win looking like that! He lost before he teed off.

At the time, I was on fire, and we had a Cheesecake Factory tournament at Los Verdes Golf Course. So all the managers wanted the owner, David Overton, to sponsor me. I was playing with him. I birdied 1, parred 2 and 3, and went to 4. It was a long par 4 with a blind second shot. I got a 3 iron out and striped it! David was at the top of the hill, and I said, "Where did it go?" He said it went in the hole and just walked on. Oh my god. So the next hole was a par 3; and I stuffed a 5 iron inside a foot, shot sixty-seven, and got no sponsor. He didn't care.

The thing about this time was that I was unhappy. I had everything except for the one thing that I wanted. Stupid! I wish that I had enjoyed the ride more.

It was my senior season. At our home tournament dinner with all the teams there, our knucklehead coach was talking, and no one was listening. I was laughing! This guy was such a bonehead. He didn't have the tee times set, so he told the coaches to call after dinner. He gave UC Irvine a time. Well, they showed up, and he gave them the wrong time and was trying to DQ them. I had to step in at this point and say, "You can't do that, Coach." Are you kidding me? So when this idiot was done talking, then came Scotty, and you could hear a pin drop. What he said was, "Smell the roses." All we could think about was being the next Nicklaus. I wish I had enjoyed it more. Two days later, on the first tee, my coach came up to me and told me Scotty had passed.

Everything that could go wrong did. I did have some good times and won a couple of tournaments. But I was playing with rabbit ears. That was what Mike called going on a date with empty pockets. If you pull out the pocket, it looks like rabbit ears. Get it? Lost luggage, lost glasses, and a sponsor pullout. The worst was that I was going to Australia to try to qualify for the tour with Tim Loustalot. The night before the flight, I had his girlfriend's car. I went out to dinner and came out to no car. It was stolen along with everything in it. It just ended up in one big mess. Then we went to Jamaica, and guess what? No luggage or clubs. No kidding! Funny sidenote: It was always funny going to a casino with Tim, and his last name always got a few laughs.

One of the highlights was that after my sponsor dropped me after the Jamaica disaster, I went back to work at the Cheesecake Factory and planned for revenge. So months before the tournament, I paid for everything—airfare, hotel, tournament fee, etc. No pressure, right? Four rounds, no cut. On the first day, I was four over, going into nine. I put the ball in a greenside bunker and proceeded to play ping-pong with another bunker. I made a thirty-footer for triple, forty-three. At this point, I was having an emotional breakdown. I was about to walk off the golf course, thinking that this was a really bad idea. The conditions were difficult, and somehow I shot thirty-four on the back seventy-seven. Seventy-three was leading. I was only four shots off the lead and two hours earlier. I was about to get on an airplane home, crying. I finished in ninth place, got a nice check, and had a great week.

Also, at this time, I got a job opening up Bighorn Golf Club in Palm Desert—all fun! The late Donnie Cude put together a great staff. We had *so* much fun. There was nothing but a golf course and a trailer. For a while, we didn't even have members. It was our club. I had *so* much fun playing as a kid. I could compete with Sam Randolph and Dennis Paulson and guys like Duffy Waldorf. I think I played my best golf then. It didn't matter how much money you had or who your daddy was. On Monday morning, we were all equal.

College was different in *so* many ways. We had no scholarships. I paid my way through college by bussing tables. There is no way you could do that today. My first semester was in the fall of '81. I took eighteen units, and it cost $116. Got a 3.85 GPA—not bad for a guy who, six months earlier, failed high school English. Golf was still free! It was hard being on a team, but we had some really fun times too.

There was nothing really fun about playing professional golf. Now it mattered how much money you had and who your daddy was. It was not fun anymore. I quit.

* ★ *

# MARATHON MAN

So somehow, through this whole mess, I found running. I could take out all my frustration by running!

I met Carl Lewis at Santa Monica High School. The Santa Monica track club ran there. Florence Griffith Joyner, Jackie Joyner-Kersee, and twenty gold medals at the Olympics—not bad. I had the same spirit for running! I wasn't fast, but I could go forever like the Energizer Bunny. So I was working at the Cheesecake Factory and running five or six miles a day every day except Sundays. I loved it! I'd crank up Van Halen and go fly. A fellow waiter, Rolland, ran marathons and told me that if what I said was true, then I could do it. No-freakin'-way! I took up his challenge. The funny thing is that when I was growing up, I figured I was going to be the next Nicklaus. I never thought that I was capable of graduating from college or running a marathon, let alone four of them. Funny how things turn out.

Okay, the game was on! I asked Rolland what was important, and he said, "Your feet, and get your weight as low as possible." Sidenote: Remember Capt. Dan in *Forrest Gump*? "Two things, boys! One, take good care of your feet, and two, try not to do anything stupid!"

Somehow, I posted up at three hours and thirty-six minutes. I was hooked. Next year, I broke three and a half hours—three hours and twenty-nine minutes—flying. The year after, it was three hours and thirty-three minutes on the number. I got burned out! That is why my last one came eleven years later.

I will talk about my brush with death later from a deadly bacteria, but what happened when I was twenty-six is worth mentioning.

It was a wet morning, and I drove to the UCLA track. I was actually running around the track that day with Carl Lewis. On my way back to Santa Monica, on Sunset Boulevard, coming around the last corner and before I crossed the 405, the back of the car slipped a little. At that point, I realized my seat belt wasn't on. I put it on, crossed the 405, and ten seconds later, the car in front of me veered right. Some guy was spinning across the road. I never saw him till I T-boned him at sixty miles an hour. Like I have said in this book, I have <u>always</u> believed in God. It wasn't my day.

I was flying! By mile 17, I came through a four-way intersection with thousands of people going nuts, even a marching band. I was right behind the leaders. I gave them a fist pump (I was listening to Van Halen's song "Dreams"). My feet felt like they were not even touching the ground. It was the greatest moment of my life. Somehow I closed in at three hours and thirty minutes. Nobody will ever understand what that means to me. I hit the wall and finished on time. Nice. That's the deal: you don't quit. It's going to hurt, and you know that going in.

I heard a story that some dude in Greece was at the beach and found out the enemy was coming; so he ran to the city of Marathon to warn them, saved the city, and dropped dead (26.2 miles)!

It really is *so* mental. Out of twenty-five thousand people that day, I finished 601st. I beat 97.6 percent of the people that ran that day, including the Kenyans. It's amazing what they can do.

The start of the race was interesting. I can't run without music. It takes my mind off my body. The night before, a friend loaded a bunch of songs, and my Walkman was not working. I was in a full panic. Seriously, I was thinking of not running the race. Ten seconds before they dropped the gate, John Cougar Mellencamp clicks on. The song was "R.O.C.K. in the U.S.A." Thank God. The mental thing is that you have to set goals to keep your mind occupied. Like at 13.1 miles, I was thinking one thing: *I am on my way home.*

You go through a series of highs and lows. You have to keep an even keel. It's hard sometimes because you want to take off, but you will red-line and blow the engine. What got me through that day was that at forty-two, I knew it was my last rodeo. I wanted and did finish in style.

# NECROTIZING FASCIITIS

My mother passed in 2017 at eighty-four. She had a good run. She left me $7,500 out of her savings and a trust that I got a few thousand from every year. She said she wanted me to have a second chance. At this point, my ex-wife and kids were not my responsibility. I got a great job lead at Kapalua, Hawaii, which has always been my favorite place on the planet. I landed and had seven great days, and then it happened.

*Necro*—that means "dead guess what"! I'm not going to miss one fact of what happened. Sidenote: I always thought religion was everybody's own personal right. My grandmother, the staunch Cuban Catholic woman that she was, sent me to a private school—Saint Monica's. Haha! Like that was going to fix the bad boy. I was an altar boy. But that didn't stop me from believing in God. He is the only one I answer to. This guy has had my back, no kidding. My name should be Dorothy Hamill. Somehow I have skated out of many dire situations like the night I went flying off Highway 74.

It was a very dangerous mountain road. I hit some gravel, and the back end came around. For some reason, I wasn't scared. All I could think about was Tom Cruise in *Days of Thunder* when he was about to crash and said while laughing, "This is going to hurt." I went spinning off the cliff, and all I could hear was *Bam, bam, bam!* Everything stopped. The first thing you do is make sure that you are in one piece. It looked like I was okay, but I was in one heck of a situation. I had landed in a tree, literally shish-kebabed. The tree went through the floorboard, the passenger seat, and the roof. I know one thing: if a car and a tree have a go at it, the tree wins every time. All I got was a few scratches while crawling out of the tree.

You should have seen the look on the guy's face at the tow yard. He was like "You are really alive?" Sure! I was just fine.

I flew to Maui and checked into a hostel in Lāhainā. I met this guy named Alan. We started playing tennis. I was telling him that I hadn't been in the ocean in ten years. I got caught in a nasty current and almost drowned. Somehow I got back in. Somehow he talked me into going back in the water. I just went in the shallow water. I was just floating in murky water. I was pushing off what I thought was rock. I was not familiar with coral. It's a living organism. I did not even cut my foot, but the bacteria went through my skin, unbeknownst to me.

I had dinner, went to bed, got up the next morning, and paid the girls at the front desk for the next night. The guy at the place, the manager, said, "No, you are only allowed seven days."

After a two-hour bus ride, I got to the hostel. I went to open door number 4, and the key wouldn't work. The guy said that since the key didn't work, he had to make another one. I got back on the bus and headed to the mall for dinner. I was just going to go to sleep. I noticed a black spot getting bigger but was still not getting it. Two buses left for the evening. I thought, *I will go to my room and the hospital in the morning.* Bus 1 was going to go to the hostel! I went to get on, and a drop of blood came out of my leg. I scraped it a few days earlier when playing tennis. The bus driver wouldn't let me on! I begged, but nope. Bus 2's first stop was Maui Memorial Medical Center. At this point, I was starting to get it. I walked into the ER, and twenty minutes later, I was in surgery. I had a lot to think about in those twenty minutes.

A doctor walked by, and I said, "Am I going to lose my foot?"

She cocked her head toward me with the most serious look I had ever seen and said, "We are not at that point yet."

It's the only time in my life I was truly scared. At first I was *so* mad at God. What a cruel twist of fate. Then I started begging God. Then right before I went into surgery, Carmen kicked in "fight." I did not threaten the man upstairs. All I said was, "You take my foot, You take me."

I woke up after surgery and looked down at my foot. The good news was that it was still there, but the bad news was that it was gutted—a shell with the top ripped off and a golf-ball-size something that looked like ground beef.

A doctor walked by, looked at it, and said, "that looks like it went thru a meat grinder."

Right? I was like "That's what I was thinking."

I got wheeled up to my residence for the next eighteen days. A nurse gave me a pamphlet and said, "Here is what you got."

*Necrotizing fasciitis* was in big black letters, and it said "Death and Amputation." It then said, "Immediate medical attention within 24 hours. Even with that 50 to 80 percent Death rate, 90 to 95 percent amputation."

I was lying there like a pincushion. I had needles and wires everywhere. They told me I had to go back under for a second surgery because he didn't get it all (*he* referring to master surgeon Dr. Peter Galpin. I was frightened but not of the surgery. I was not cool with being put under. So I met this man, and he was in a real wheelchair. I guess it was like flying off Highway 74. For some stupid reason, I had always felt invincible. He said, "Get your ass downstairs." I never felt so small. This man, I found out, was hit by a drunk driver and paralyzed at eighteen. One thing I learned when going through what I did is that there are a lot of people that got a bad deal worse than you (or me).

Now it was about three or four days later, and they said, "You are going to lavage," which sounds like a French bubble bath—not exactly! They had vacuumed my foot shut like a piece of salmon. The doctor was going to rip it open, clean it, and reseal it. I asked the doc, "Is this going to hurt?" Yes. It was pain that I could <u>never</u> imagine. It was bad. They gave me morphine. That shit did nothing. I had to go through this procedure six times. Eventually, I looked at my foot and saw it was ruby red. Nice job, Peter Galpin. Yes, I had no idea. Thank God for what was coming.

It was day 18. I got a pair of crutches and was tossed out the door. Seriously, though, the doctors were so amazing and kind to me; and the nurses also took a liking to me. Homeless, crippled, and almost broke—nice trifecta.

Susan helped me again. She rented a condo in Maui for eight months. I just remember having to crawl to the bathroom. Seriously, without that woman, I would not be alive. What is really cool is that is not why I love her. I call her Amelia, like the chick with the airplane. Unlike Charles Lindbergh, she had a guy in the back of the plane, a navigator. I don't want talk about what I had to go through. No matter what, we talked on the phone <u>every day</u>. That, and I would try to always put my head down in front of a church. I would tell myself, "This is 0 percent your fault! Whatever you do, do not get down on yourself." My foot is about 50 percent, but she works. I can do everything but run—a small price to pay. This book is not yet finished. This boy's journey is not done yet.

# THE PAYNE FACTOR

So all this stuff was going on in college. I was paying attention, and Payne Stewart was playing great golf. Somehow I always won when he did and played poorly at the same time he did.

I think what is really cool is that I was born on the same day: January 30. He was the big brother you never had but wanted! As I wrote on the back page, we all are connected. The year 1993 was a fun time. I was at Bighorn. We had the skins game. Payne won. I sat in the men's locker room, working, and all the press had left. Everyone had left. I looked at this guy, and it was just me and him. It was the strangest feeling I have ever had. We looked at each other, and it was eerie! It is the only time I crossed paths with him.

I want to make sure of one thing. Whatever I wrote in this book is the truth! So this gets crazy! Oh my god, I could not make this stuff up!

It was June 20, Father's Day! And it was the last round of the 1999 US Open. I was watching this battle between Phil Mickelson and Payne, and at the same time, I was in the hospital. My wife was in labor. It's hard to believe this really happened.

Nicolas was born, my only son, on Father's Day. Are you kidding? I was holding on to him in front and watching this drama between two great players at the top of their game. What a battle. As it turned out, Payne played the most amazing golf. Clutched it!

So as I was sitting there, Payne had Phil's head in his hands and said, "You are going to be a father." There's no better gift! I know that is a moment that wasn't my doing. But wow!

# 2 AMIGOS

Dr. Frank Scott, and Carmen DenDekker—these are the two people who really understood me.

Scotty—everybody loved this guy! He skated me into SDSU. I failed high school English. Just a couple of funny stories. This is one of them. He was seventy-five years old, and I was eighteen. He was the coach for forty years and "never played golf," but Scotty knew about people. We had no money and no scholarship. In the second semester of my freshman year, I lived with him and his wife, Helen. So at nighttime one day, I helped myself to his booze cabinet. I woke up at 7:00 a.m. He was laughing at me.

"You know that you have English class at 8:00 a.m.?"

Yes, I never missed one class in college. He let me run. He knew that when it came down to it, I would *always* show up.

Carmen DenDekker, my mother, did the same thing. She gave up so much to raise me and is my biggest fan. She knew how to handle me too. She knew that I would be out with the boys on Saturday night, but she also knew that I would be dressed and proper on Sunday morning for church.

# AUTHOR'S NOTE

"**A** story!"—that's all I keep hearing. People want to hear an entertaining story. If it is true, *so* much the better. I took thirty days to write chicken scratches (the manuscript). But the story was there.

Growing up, I saw life as "The one who has the most fun wins!" I cared about three things: sports, beer, and skirts (not in any particular order). I didn't try to hide it! What people didn't see was all the work I put in, like going to class with rabbit ears and silver-dollar eyeballs, running five or six miles a day for decades, or eating drive-through at 9:00 p.m. because I was practicing. Hopefully, this book brings to fact that I was paying attention.

I have been told that I write well, that I am a storyteller, that I have some very funny stories, and that I am well versed in the English language. I think it all adds up to something entertaining and true.

www.ingramcontent.com/pod-product-compliance
Lightning Source LLC
Chambersburg PA
CBHW040112150726
48005CB00013B/1663